1965 BENJAMIN F. FAIRLESS MEMORIAL LECTURES

The management of prosperity

Arthur F. Burns

Distributed by Columbia University Press
New York-London

The Benjamin F. Fairless Memorial Lectures endowment fund has been established at Carnegie Institute of Technology to support an annual series of lectures. An internationally known figure from the worlds of business, government, or education will be invited each year to present three lectures at Carnegie under the auspices of its Graduate School of Industrial Administration. In general, the lectures will be concerned with some aspects of business or public administration; the relationships between business and government, management and labor; or a subject related to the themes of preserving economic freedom, human liberty, and the strengthening of individual enterprise— all of which were matters of deep concern to Mr. Fairless throughout his career.

The lecturer will, whenever possible, spend three weeks in residence on the Carnegie Campus, during which time he will be available for discussions with faculty and students.

Mr. Fairless was president of United States Steel Corporation for fifteen years, and chairman of the board from 1952 until his retirement in 1955. A friend of Carnegie Institute of Technology for many years, he served on the board of trustees from 1952 until his death. In 1959 he was named honorary chairman of the board. He was also a leader and co-chairman of Carnegie Tech's ten-year development program, from its beginning in 1957.

239450

1965

seven

Dr. Arthur F. Burns is President of the National Bureau of Economic Research, Inc., and is the John Bates Clark Professor of Economics at Columbia University. He received his A.B., A.M., and Ph.D. degrees from Columbia and is the recipient of twelve honorary degrees.

He was Chairman of the President's Council of Economic Advisers from 1953 through 1956 under President Eisenhower. He has also served at various times as a consultant to the Treasury Department, the National Security Council, the Department of Defense, the Department of State, the Labor Department, the Federal Reserve Board, and other governmental agencies. He is currently a member of the President's Advisory Committee on Labor-Management Policy. In 1959 he was President of the American Economic Association.

I. Our longest expansion

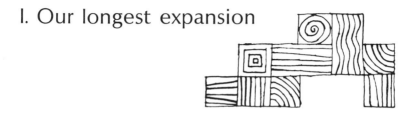

I. Our longest expansion

In the course of the campaign of 1960, Senator John F. Kennedy promised that if he were elected president, America would get moving again. This promise or prophecy has been amply fulfilled in the economic sphere—which is my sole concern on this occasion. In the three years preceding the campaign, our economy made little progress in expanding production or employment. From the summer of 1957 to the spring of 1958 we experienced a recession which, although moderate by pre-war standards, was the sharpest of the post-war period. The recovery that followed was fairly strong at the outset, but it soon faltered and did not return the nation to full prosperity. In the spring of 1960 the economy again lapsed into recession and, while the decline was extremely mild, unemployment mounted and reached seven per cent in the spring of 1961.

As was generally expected, the new administration embarked promptly on an expansionist economic policy. In February 1961, just one month after it took up the reins of government, economic recovery started. It is very doubtful, however, whether this development can be credited to the new administration. Judging from the national income accounts, the decline of 1960-61 came as close to being a pure inventory recession as any on record. In the first quarter of 1960 business firms in the aggregate added to their inventories at an annual rate of ten billion dollars. A year later they cut back inventories at an annual rate of three and a half billion dollars. This turnaround of 13 billion dollars in inventory investment reflected readjustments in steel and various other industries, but it was not accompanied by any over-all decline of demand. On the contrary, the demand of final buyers, both domestic and foreign, kept growing during the recession, quarter after quarter. In these circumstances, the decline of inventories relative to sales could not long continue. Once the level of inventories again approached the desired relationship to sales, a recovery in orders and production followed naturally. The substantial easing of credit by the Federal Reserve authorities during 1960 doubtless played some part in maintaining aggregate demand and thereby hastening the end of the inventory adjustment; this, I am inclined to believe, is about all that governmental intervention accomplished at this stage.

But if the new administration cannot be credited with initiating the revival, it did assume a very active role during the process of recovery and in turning what might have been an ordinary expansion into a remarkable upsurge of the economy. During its course, the nation's real output of goods and services has increased at an average annual rate of over five per cent, total employment has grown by about six million, profits have improved handsomely, and the unemployment rate has declined from about seven per cent to four and a half per cent. Meanwhile, the level of wholesale prices remained stable for several years, and even the advance of consumer prices slowed down. More impressive still, the current expansion has already lasted 56 months, and still appears to have momentum. Reasonably accurate records for the past hundred and some years disclose no other peacetime expansion that lasted so long. To find a longer stretch of sustained advance, it is necessary to go back to the expansion of 1938-45, which spanned World War II, or else turn to Western Europe where the business cycle has tended, historically, to run longer than in our country and where, in the post-war period, long intervals of sustained expansion have become commonplace.

It is characteristic of a prolonged period of growth that it excites hopeful speculation about the future. This is particularly true when, as in the current case, boldness and innovation have marked the course of governmental economic policy—witness the investment tax credit, the liberalized depreciation rules, the succession of tax cuts, the guideposts for prices and wages, the interest equalization tax, the voluntary program for restricting foreign loans and investments, medicare for the aged, new housing subsidies, the anti-poverty program, and so on. On the whole, the American people appear to have reacted to these measures of policy with a sense of admiration of the ingenuity with which our economic prosperity is being managed. If some citizens, clinging to older beliefs about the proper role of government, have been fearful that every new stimulant of the economy is merely paving the way for a new and perhaps drastic economic decline, there are many others who now dare to believe that the business cycle has been mastered and that our governmental authorities already have the knowledge as well as the power to extend prosperity indefinitely.

I cannot hope in the course of this lecture to give a full or entirely just account of the current expansion. Such an assessment requires a degree of personal detachment and historical perspective that few, if any, current observers are capable of achieving. I shall try, however, to analyze some of the causes of the remarkable expansion of economic activity that we have been experiencing and to draw a lesson or two that may perhaps prove useful to our nation in the future.

One factor underlying the sustained expansion has undoubtedly been the willingness of the federal government to pursue a liberal fiscal policy, and to support it with as much monetary ease as the state of our balance of payments might allow. The principle of balancing the budget annually had already been abandoned years earlier. In fact, no serious attempt was made to resurrect it even during the Republican regime of the fifties. The principle that took its place was that of the compensatory budget, which required rough budgetary balance over the period of a business cycle, instead of every year. Under this rule, governmental deficits could be run during a recession and also in the early stage of recovery, but not when expansion was already well under way. President Kennedy adhered to this principle at the outset, but later moved to the bolder policy advocated by his Council of Economic Advisers—namely, the deliberate adoption of budgetary deficits without regard to their duration or the stage of the business cycle, as long as a gap existed between the nation's actual production and what it theoretically could produce if unemployment did not exceed four per cent. This, in a sentence, is the essence of what is nowadays frequently referred to as the "new economics."

Steady reliance on a liberal fiscal policy, whether through increased spending or lower taxes, thus became the keystone of the administration's economic program. This policy requires that the government put more money into the economy than it takes out, and this has been our practice since early 1961. During the entire course of the expansion, except for the second quarter of this year, when tax receipts piled up beyond expectations, the federal cash budget has shown a deficit. This experience is quite different from the earlier post-war expansions, when surpluses were interspersed with deficits. The cumulative deficit since the first quarter of 1961 has therefore been climbing steadily and already amounts to about 23 billion dollars, in contrast to a surplus of 300 million during the expansion of 1949-53, which spanned the costly Korean war; a surplus of four billion during the expansion of 1954-57; and a deficit of 13.5 billion accumulated during the incomplete expansion of 1958-60. Thus, it is entirely clear that deficit finance has played a larger and more consistent role in the present expansion than in any of its immediate predecessors.

Moreover, the monetary policy of the past few years has given strong support to the liberal fiscal policy despite the chronic imbalance in our international transactions. To be sure, short-term rates of interest in the open market, as well as the interest rates paid by banks on time deposits, were permitted to rise in order to restrain the outflow of short-term capital. However, the monetary authorities saw to it that the commercial banks were supplied abundantly with reserves, so that both bank credit and the money supply could grow briskly. Free reserves of commercial banks remained positive during the first four years of the current expansion, in contrast to earlier experience when they turned negative after a year or two of expansion. Throughout this expansion, bank credit—that is, the sum of loans and investments of commercial banks—has risen at an annual rate that remained close to eight or nine per cent. In earlier post-war expansions the rate of growth of bank credit, besides being much lower, tended to slow down after a year or two. The rate of growth of the nation's money supply—that is, currency in public circulation plus deposits in commercial banks—has likewise been higher and steadier than in the preceding expansions. And although short-term market rates of interest have risen appreciably since 1961, the abundance of reserves in the hands of commercial bankers has served to keep the interest rates that matter most for the domestic economy at moderate levels. As late as mid-1965, high-grade corporate bond yields were still approximately at the same level as at the bottom of the recession in 1961. So too were short-term interest rates ordinarily charged by banks on business loans; while mortgage yields, municipal bond yields, and bond yields of lower grade corporate issues were actually below their recession levels.

The essential feature of economic policy in the past few years has thus been the application of fiscal stimuli in a context of monetary ease. The success that has apparently accompanied the energetic pursuit of this policy has given rise to the view, put crisply by a member of the Council of Economic Advisers, that "we know how to create jobs." The thought is that when the government applies "general fiscal stimulus," and supports it by easy credit, "the normal working of our private economy is able to create jobs for our growing labor force." This view merits some pondering, whether we take it as a generalization based on the recent past or as a prescription for the future.

It is well to recall, first of all, that although fiscal deficits and monetary ease have ruled since early 1961, the course of our economic expansion has been quite uneven. During its first year, plans for federal spending were repeatedly revised upward, and actual expenditures followed suit. The annual rate of federal cash payments to the public rose seven billion dollars between the first quarter of 1961 and the first quarter of 1962. Consumer spending and inventory investment also increased materially. However, business investment in plant and equipment remained sluggish, and failed to display any signs of soon developing the vigor that is characteristic of economic recovery. By the first quarter of 1962, new orders and contracts for plant and equipment were merely 13 per cent higher than a year earlier, in contrast to increases of 68 per cent, 54 per cent, and 28 per cent during the corresponding stage of the three preceding expansions. Unemployment diminished, but its rate of decline was abnormally slow. Clearly, the recovery was not proceeding as had been hoped, despite the vigorous fiscal and monetary stimuli that were being applied. The weak link in the chain of economic recovery was private investment in fixed capital; and

seventeen

the reason most often advanced for its sluggishness—namely, that industry was burdened with considerable excess capacity when the recovery started—provided little comfort, since this condition was bound to continue for some time.

In fact, this explanation missed the essence of what was happening. It is true that excess capacity existed on a considerable scale in 1961, as it always does in the neighborhood of a recession. But, as far as I know, excess capacity has never prevented a rapid increase of business capital investment when a resurgence of confidence ushered in economic recovery. The historical record indicates that business investment in fixed capital rebounded sharply even after prolonged or severe contractions of economic activity, when excess capacity was of course much larger than in 1961. For example, the depression of the 1870's reached bottom in 1878, and business investment the following year rose 24 per cent. The depression of the 1880's reached bottom in 1885, and business investment the following year rose 35 per cent. Again, business investment in 1922 was 20 per cent above the level of 1921. These are not isolated examples. On the contrary, they express what is a normal feature of the early stage of a business-cycle expansion. Despite the excess capacity that emerges during an economic slump, investment commitments tend to rise briskly once confidence returns. New firms are then established in larger numbers and they undertake new investments; existing firms in turn speed investments that are associated with innovation; firms that have done well despite the slump proceed to enlarge their capacity in anticipation of stronger demand; while many of the firms that have fallen behind in the competitive race finally undertake substantial programs of improvement or modernization.

It was not overcapacity, but rather the want of sufficient confidence, that kept investment from expanding more vigorously during 1961. The coming of a new administration that was strongly supported by the trade union movement inevitably raised questions in the minds of businessmen who were already concerned about the steady rise of labor costs and the erosion of profit margins during the late fifties. Some businessmen feared that governmental spending and deficits would increase rapidly, that trade unions would become bolder in their wage demands, and that either a price inflation or a diminution of profits would be the consequence. Others, more immersed in the international aspects of business, feared that liberal fiscal and monetary policies would lead to further deterioration in the balance of payments and threaten the external value of the dollar. Still others feared that the country would refuse to tolerate a protracted series of fiscal deficits and that new taxes might soon be added to the heavy tax load that corporations and individual investors were already carrying, or else that the government might move toward direct controls over prices in order to contain the inflationary pressures that resulted from its monetary and fiscal policies. These strands of thought crossed one another in countless patterns of anxiety. Economists or political philosophers may find it interesting to speculate whether this or that view was justified. What matters from the viewpoint of plain history is that many businessmen were deeply troubled, and that not a few among them deemed it prudent to delay investment commitments until governmental policies clarified.

The fears of the business community reached a climax in April 1962 when President Kennedy moved sternly to force the major steel companies to rescind the price increase that they had just posted. This action by the President had no clear sanction in law and it caused consternation in business circles. Men reasoned that if the government could coerce or punish the steel industry today, it might move next against the automobile industry or the chemical industry or any other. Since the beginning of 1962 economic recovery had shown some signs of hesitation. Now, with confidence shaken, its continuance became much more doubtful. The stock market reflected the mood of the time by experiencing its sharpest break of the entire post-war period. Orders for machinery, equipment, and other goods were cut back here and there. New business incorporations declined, and so too did appropriations by manufacturing firms for capital expenditures. Private borrowing diminished, the layoff rate rose a little, unemployment stopped declining, raw material prices softened, profit margins narrowed, and large business bankruptcies became more numerous. The index of industrial pro-

nineteen

duction, which had risen smartly until April 1962, flattened out for the rest of the year. The gross national product still continued to rise, but its rate of advance became lower. In short, the economy became sluggish in 1962, particularly in the second half of the year.

Fortunately, an imminent recession was forestalled. President Kennedy had a quick and honest mind. Recognizing that the government's handling of the steel price problem had disturbed and estranged the business community, he turned at once to the difficult task of rebuilding confidence. In one pronouncement after another, the President and other high officials now sought to convey that what had happened in the case of steel was in no sense a harbinger of direct price or profit controls. By stressing the vital role of free markets and of profits in generating economic growth, these pronouncements helped to reassure the business community. However, once confidence has been shaken, it cannot be restored promptly or by verbal reassurances alone. Scepticism among businessmen lingered on until it became quite plain that the government was seeking to create a better environment for business enterprise.

Constructive actions were not long delayed. The Treasury, which had been wrestling for many months with the problem of depreciation, announced in July 1962 that business firms could henceforth reckon their income taxes on the basis of shorter and more realistic lives of depreciable facilities. This depreciation reform meant substantial immediate tax savings. It had long been sought unsuccessfully by corporate executives, and they could not fail to note that a Democratic administration did something for the business world that a Republican administration had staunchly refused. Nor was liberalized depreciation the only tax benefit extended to the business community. With the President's prodding, the Congress enacted an investment tax credit which had already been proposed in 1961, but which was now modified in ways that made it more acceptable to businessmen. And in the late summer of 1962 the President made his boldest move. Since early 1958, when public discussion of tax policy got seriously under way, many businessmen and economists had been urging a reduction of income tax rates.

Certainly, the stiff federal tax on personal incomes, particularly in the upper brackets, and also the heavy tax on corporate profits were a legacy of the Great Depression and World War II, when there was little or no interest in encouraging private investment. Whatever their merit may have been at other times, these taxes were now inhibiting economic growth. The President was well informed of the movement for tax reform, and he was also aware of the ingenious tax policies that other industrial countries had been pursuing in post-war years to promote expansion of their economies. In view of the precarious state of confidence and his own growing conviction that our tax system had become a drag on enterprise and investment, he announced in August 1962 his intention to achieve a substantial and sweeping reduction of income tax rates—a reduction that would apply to individuals throughout the income range and to corporations as well as to individuals. In January 1963, the President made specific recommendations along these lines to the Congress.

The new tone of governmental economic pronouncements, and even more the new tax policies, had a wholesome effect on business and investor sentiment. Fears of hostile governmental intervention in the day-by-day activities of business firms gradually subsided. Businessmen, and indeed the public at large, began viewing the economic future a little more cheerfully. True, a substantial part of the business community did not like the budgetary implications of a tax cut at a time when governmental spending was rising and a sizable deficit was already in the making. But while some business executives opposed tax reduction to the bitter end, many others were quick to see that stimulation of the economy by fiscal devices, whether appropriate or not, had become practically unavoidable. This being the case, lower taxes were clearly preferable to additional public spending, since they would serve to expand the private sector of the economy instead of adding further to the government's command over the nation's resources. Not only that, lower tax rates meant a better environment for risk-taking and investment. With lower tax rates, there would be some tendency to curb public expenditures and the private economy might expand so rapidly that public revenues would soon match expenditures

twenty-one

once again. In any event, lower tax rates meant more money in the pocketbook today and perhaps also tomorrow. Thus, the new twist of fiscal policy helped to rebuild confidence.

So too did other developments. Powerful though economic motives are, other psychological forces inevitably leave their mark on economic behavior. Certainly, the President's firmness in handling the Cuban missile crisis in the fall of 1962 made Americans feel better about themselves and their country, and thereby added something to the energy with which people went about their daily business. Meanwhile, the sluggishness of general business activity kept releasing forces that favored a resumption of economic growth, in much the same way that a recession normally lays the basis for new expansion. Here and there inventories were being readjusted, so that new orders would soon need to reflect actual sales. Also, since cancellations were relatively few, the backlog of investment projects tended to grow with every postponement. The stock market was already well deflated. Lenders were hunting for customers, and long-term interest rates were dropping. With these developments under way and optimism reviving, conditions were ripe for a new wave of expansion. By the end of 1962, business commitments for investment in fixed capital began rising once again, and fears of an early recession soon vanished.

The momentous shift of fiscal policy from heavier spending to tax reduction came gradually. The President's fiscal program, as announced early in 1963, called for an increase of budget expenditures of four and a half billion dollars, besides a net tax reduction estimated at over ten billion dollars. In the following months, this fiscal program was extensively discussed and debated. The proposal for tax reduction quickly won powerful and wide support. Considerable resistance developed, however, within Congress as well as the business community to a simultaneous reduction of taxes and increase of spending. This was sharply conveyed by the preamble of the House tax bill, which Congressman Wilbur Mills, the author of the preamble, described as "a firm, positive assertion" that the nation is choosing tax reduction, and rejecting larger spending, as its "road to a bigger, more progressive economy." President Kennedy assented to this preamble as well as to the substantive provisions of the bill; but final passage was delayed until early 1964 when the Congress had already been officially advised by the new President, Mr. Johnson, that the planned cash outlays of the federal government for the following fiscal year were no larger than in the current year and that the expenditures planned under the administrative budget were actually 500 million dollars lower.

In all, about a year and a half elapsed between President Kennedy's first announcement of the plan for a general tax reduction and its actual enactment. The benefits, however, came sooner. As the legislation worked its way through the halls of Congress, more and more citizens came to feel that lower personal and corporate income taxes would soon be legislated. Since the income at the disposal of their families or businesses would soon be larger, they in effect already had a greater incentive to work and to spend or invest. Thus, the growing expectation of a tax cut stimulated some consumers to spend more boldly, and encouraged business firms to plan or undertake larger investments in new plant and equipment. The conservative preamble to the tax bill gave a further lift to business sentiment, and so too did President Johnson's judicious handling of the office that he inherited in an hour of tragedy and sorrow that will never be forgotten. President Johnson's first budget soon supplied new and more tangible evidence that our nation's fiscal policy was really changing; that, while remaining expansionist, it now sought to achieve expansion through the private sector of the economy instead of the public sector. In later months President Johnson gave further proof of the new mood of frugality, either by announcing cuts in expenditure or by indicating that the new policy of tax reduction will be continued. Businessmen responded warmly to the new direction of economic policy. They liked President Johnson's businesslike manner, they drew encouragement from his economic pronouncements, and they felt good about many of the new appointments he made. Thus, President Johnson completed with extraordinary skill the task of rebuilding confidence that President Kennedy courageously started and carried forward a considerable way.

twenty-three

It may seem natural to attribute the durability of our expansion since 1961 to the willingness to finance the federal establishment by running deficits, year after year. It may seem natural to credit the massive reduction of income taxes with this achievement. It may seem natural to hold that the sustained expansion which we have been experiencing was so planned by governmental authorities. Such explanations, however, are only partial truths. The economy did not respond, as expected, to deficit spending during the first year or two of this expansion. The economy rebounded with vigor in 1963, many months before the deficits planned through tax reduction became effective. The steel price episode of April 1962 was not planned by anyone, and yet it released forces and counterforces that—in the end—contributed materially to prolonging the expansion. Even if we consider only the period since 1963, it was not the tax reduction as such but rather its balanced character, and still more fundamentally the improving environment for private enterprise of which the tax legislation was itself a symptom, that more than any other single factor accounts for the boom that our nation has been experiencing. This, I think, is the most important lesson to be derived from the current expansion.

It is not, however, the only lesson, any more than fiscal deficits or tax cuts or easy credit are the only cause of what is already our longest peacetime expansion. If business investment in plant and equipment was sluggish at the start of the expansion, that also helped to leave room, so to speak, for more vigorous activity later. If investment both in fixed capital and in inventories was checked in 1962, that too contributed to greater activity later. If the shift toward public policies that were more mindful of business interests took place gradually, that in its turn helped to keep the spread of business optimism from spilling over into exuberance. The fact is that, although our current expansion has been exceptionally long, it has by no means been exceptionally rapid or intense. This feature of moderation accounts in considerable degree for the postponement, if not the prevention, of serious imbalances between inventories and sales, or between industrial capacity and production, or between prices and unit costs of production, any of which could by now have brought on a recession.

Until recently, inflationary pressures have been slight in our commodity and labor markets. As late as 1964, the average level of wholesale prices was no higher than it had been in 1959 or 1960. The labor cost per unit of output in manufacturing was actually a little lower on the average, and so too were long-term interest rates. In this environment of relative stability of costs and prices, there was little reason to accumulate inventories as a hedge against inflation. Nor was there any need to rush investments in fixed capital on the ground that costs of construction or of equipment or of financing were likely to be appreciably higher next year than now. On the other hand, with profit margins tending to improve and the physical volume of business also advancing, there was sufficient incentive after 1962 to expand business capital investment at a pace which, while by no means spectacular, was still satisfactory. Thus the relative stability of costs and prices favored quietly and unobtrusively the continuance of expansion. Effective though fiscal stimuli and monetary ease undoubtedly were in sustaining the expansion of the economy, they could hardly have achieved their purpose if inflation had again raised its head. As it was, the stability of the wholesale price level served to keep speculative excesses from developing on a significant scale. Also, with much of the rest of the world practicing inflation once again, our stable prices stimulated exports sufficiently to enable us to stumble along without a balance of payments crisis; and they made expansionist economic policies far more acceptable than would have been the case if inflationary pressures were being keenly felt.

The circumstances that made it possible for our wholesale price level to remain stable so long are therefore important to an understanding of the current expansion. One stabilizing force came from abroad. Of late, many foreign manufacturers have gained the benefit of an advanced technology besides that of low-priced labor, and they have therefore been able to offer increasingly stiff competition to domestic producers of steel, textiles, machinery, radios, television sets, transport equipment, optical supplies, and many other goods. Other stabilizing forces

twenty-five

were of domestic origin. The improvement of productivity proceeded somewhat faster after 1960 than in the preceding quinquennium, and this made it easier for business firms to pay higher wages per hour without incurring higher costs per unit of output. Also, governmental exhortation with regard to prices and wages, while frequently defied, may have had some stabilizing influence on the price level. But far more important than any of these influences has been the moderate slack of industrial capacity and the moderately large unemployment of recent years, and this fundamental cause in turn has its historical roots.

With few interruptions our nation has practiced inflation since the early 1930's. For a while, after the Korean bulge, wholesale and consumer prices stabilized, but wages still kept rising faster than productivity, so that labor costs per unit of output continued to climb. As the economy approached full employment again in 1955, the level of wholesale prices joined the advance of unit labor costs and the economy boomed until mid-1957. In the recession that followed, aggregate demand declined materially. That, however, did not halt the inflation; on the contrary, both wages and prices continued to rise ominously. In the spring of 1958, economic activity began to recover once again; but even before that, equities were bid up swiftly on the stock exchanges — a development that suggested that investors expected inflation to continue. The fact that governmental expenditures undertaken to check the recession were paving the way for a peacetime fiscal deficit of unprecedented magnitude added to concern about inflation. Meanwhile, our balance of payments had turned seriously adverse. Over two billion dollars of gold left the country in 1958, and foreign financiers began to express uneasiness about our nation's ability or willingness to halt inflation.

It was in this setting that President Eisenhower decided that strong measures were needed if the inflationary psychology, which had been built up over the years, was to be curbed before it caused lasting damage to our economy and to our international political position. Between the first quarter of 1959 and the second quarter of 1960 the federal cash budget shifted from a deficit at an annual rate of 15 billion dollars to a surplus of five billion dollars, and this enormous fiscal swing was accompanied by sharp monetary restraints. Much may be said in criticism of the restrictive economic policy of that time — that it was too abrupt and was carried to excess, that it served to bring the expansion that started in 1958 to a premature end, that too much unemployment existed when the economy reached its fragile peak in the spring of 1960, and that unemployment rose still further during the recession that followed. All this and perhaps more may be fairly said. But it is also worth remembering that the highly restrictive policy of 1959 and early 1960 served a historic function: that it routed a dangerous inflationary psychology, that it demonstrated that ours need not be an age of inflation, that it stimulated businessmen to cut costs and to eliminate wasteful practices that had grown up in an inflationary environment, and that it thus laid the foundation for the long stretch of expansion that we have been experiencing. With the slack of industrial capacity serving as a brake on prices, and with moderately large unemployment helping to keep wage increases from outrunning the improvement of productivity in the manner that they had in earlier years, our economy has been able to move forward without exciting the speculative developments that frequently bring expansion to an early close. Even as markets became tighter, the earlier collapse of inflationary expectations continued for a time to exercise a restraining influence on the market behavior of both businessmen and labor leaders.

Thus the current expansion, like earlier periods of prosperity, has been a product of many causes. Indeed, this expansion might be viewed as being merely the longest of a run of rather long expansions — itself a result in some part of the vast growth of the service industries, tighter control over inventories, and other structural changes of our economy in this generation. If the economic stimulus of fiscal deficits has helped to smooth the path of our policymakers since 1961, so too did the psychology of confidence once they made it their ally. If governmental officials have left their mark on the course of events, so too have the millions of consumers, businessmen, workers, and their representatives. If the "new economics" has contributed much

twenty-seven

to the expansion, the "old economics" too has made its con-tribution. And if some advocates of the "old economics" have yet to learn that fiscal deficits and monetary ease will not always produce inflation, so too must some of the advocates of the "new economics" still learn that their favorite instruments of policy, if pushed beyond a point, may readily bring on inflation and undermine prosperity.

That point may be close at hand, if it has not already been reached. The slack of industrial capacity that existed several years ago has now been sharply reduced. In December 1963, manufacturing industries, taken in the aggregate, operated at 85 per cent of capacity. In December 1964, the percentage was 88—or merely four points below the reported optimum rate. Currently, the operating rate must be as high or higher. More-over, these figures are averages and therefore conceal the fact that manufacturers in numerous industries have for some time been operating at or above their own optimum rates. Unem-ployment has also declined substantially, and is now largely concentrated among unskilled and inexperienced workers. As far as skilled labor is concerned, shortages have become exten-sive. With demand pressing increasingly on the supply of re-sources, wholesale prices are no longer steady and the advance of consumer prices is quickening. Prices of raw materials began advancing toward the end of 1963; but the over-all index of wholesale prices still stood at 100, on a 1957-59 base, as late as June 1964. Since then, price increases in wholesale markets have spread out over the economy, and the index has risen three per cent. In recent months, the advance in wages has also shown a tendency to accelerate. Despite improvements in productivity, the labor cost per unit of output has begun to creep up in manufacturing, and it has done more than that for some time outside of manufacturing. These developments, together with the booming rates of investment in numerous industries, indi-cations of overbuilding in the housing market, and various symptoms of deterioration in the quality of credit, are a warning that the business cycle is not yet dead.

The immediate task of managing prosperity has therefore be-come more exacting. It is one thing for an economy to advance steadily when it is operating at some distance from full employment. It is quite another to continue expanding when it is already operating at or close to full employment. Now that we are approaching the latter stage, the liberal monetary and fiscal policy that our government is still pursuing is likely to intensify upward pressures on both wages and prices. True, interest rates on long-term as well as short-term loans have risen modestly since mid-year, but the surging demand for credit has swamped the influence of higher interest rates and the expansion of bank credit is continuing at a very rapid rate. Meanwhile, the curve of federal spending, which had flattened out for a year and a half, is again moving sharply upward—in part, but by no means entirely, because of rising military costs in Vietnam. If these financial conditions continue, the extraordinary expansion of our economy since 1961—which has done so much to lift the hopes of millions of our people—may come to an inglorious end. With an inflationary psychology again spreading, the danger of overstocking or overbuilding can no longer be remote. Nor is our balance of payments in a good position to withstand another round of inflation. While a change of economic policy always involves some risk, I believe that the managers of our national prosperity will have the best chance of extending the current expansion if they will, on the one hand, deal more realistically with the structural causes of unemployment and, on the other, take steps to slow down the rate of growth of bank credit and curb for a while the increase in federal spending on civilian programs.

October 26, 1965

twenty-nine

II. The problem of unemployment

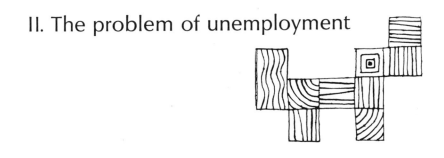

II. The problem of unemployment

In the preceding lecture I attempted to analyze some of the causes of the extraordinary expansion in economic activity that we have experienced since early 1961. Clearly, this has been a period of increasing abundance and prosperity. Production, both in the aggregate and on a per capita basis, has risen substantially and with little interruption. The like has been true of employment, the flow of incomes, consumer buying, and corporate profits. Our growing prosperity, moreover, has been shared widely by the nation's families, communities, and businesses. And yet, the good times of recent years have been clouded by unemployment. Although the rate of unemployment has gradually diminished, it has consistently remained above four per cent—that is, above the "interim target" which the managers of our national prosperity have set for implementing a full employment policy. To find an unemployment rate as low as two or three per cent, it is necessary to go back to the decade preceding the recession of 1953-54. To find an unemployment rate as low as four per cent, it is necessary to go back to the boom of 1956 and early 1957. In 1964, our best year since then, unemployment averaged 5.2 per cent. And although the unemployment rate has moved below five per cent this year, it was still nearly 4.5 per cent at the time of the most recent survey.

The persistence of sizable unemployment in the midst of increasing prosperity has been a disquieting experience to thoughtful Americans. An unemployment rate of four and a half or five per cent is high for any country, and it is uncomfortably high for a nation that aspires to greatness. For that very reason, it is important to approach our unemployment problem searchingly and yet guard against exaggeration.

An unemployment rate of, let us say, five per cent does not mean, as social critics sometimes suggest, that one out of twenty breadwinners is anxiously pacing the streets in search of any sort of job to enable him to feed his family. Taken as a whole, unemployed workers in our country are neither a static nor an impoverished group. Normally, a high proportion of those who are unemployed in a particular month are either working again or are out of the labor force the following month. Most unemployed men with family responsibilities manage to find jobs within a few weeks. Moreover, they usually can draw unemployment insurance or dip into their savings while looking for work. A large fraction of the unemployed consists of married women, teenagers, or pensioners, who often wish only part-time or intermittent work. Not a few of the unemployed have given up their jobs to search for better opportunities or a different style of living. Some of the unemployed actually have a job but have not as yet reported for work, or are absent from their present job while looking for another, or are waiting to be recalled when the temporary shutdown of the plant where they work, lasting perhaps two or three weeks, has ended. On the other hand, some of those counted as employed are doing temporary or part-time work when they would much prefer to have regular full-time jobs.

We may draw at once two inferences from these facts. First, minor and not unreasonable adaptations of unemployment figures may change their look. For example, if all those having a job were omitted from the unemployment count, and if the unemployment figure itself were expressed as a percentage of the total labor force including the armed forces, instead of the civilian labor force alone as is customary, the unemployment rate would be lowered by about a half of one per cent; that is, an unemployment rate of five per cent would usually become 4.4 or 4.5 per cent. Second, the reported unemployment for any month or year does not tell us nearly enough either about the waste of resources or about the human cost that is connected with unemployment. To deal with the unemployment problem intelligently, it is necessary to know what types of people are unemployed and how strenuously they may be looking for jobs.

We are on safer ground in making relative comparisons of unemployment over time, but even here we must be cautious. Although our statistics of unemployment have been compiled on a virtually uniform basis during the post-war years, they are insensitive to gradual changes in the character of unemployment. One of the telling advantages that wealth brings to an individual or to a family is a widening of choice. Clearly, a relatively poor man is under greater pressure to take a job than a man of substantial means. The former may need to settle on a job promptly, while the latter can bide his time and explore opportunities more thoroughly. And what is true of men is even more true of their wives and children. Unless supplementary income is needed to provide the necessities of life, the main breadwinner is likely to encourage his wife to hold out for a job that is reasonably attractive, and he is especially likely to urge his son to look for a post that has something of a future. But if the growth of individual and family incomes has tended to make people more selective about jobs, it has for that very reason tended to lengthen the usual interval of unemployment. The spread of unemployment insurance, and more liberal welfare programs generally, have also worked in that direction. The great merit of these social measures is that they maintain the flow of income on a modest scale even during periods of unemployment, so that even poor men may practice some of the discrimination in job choosing that comes as a matter of course to the well-to-do. Our statistical measures, however, do not recognize this voluntary aspect of unemployment, nor the fact that our growing prosperity and social legislation are tending to increase it.

Another factor that needs to be considered is the changing structure of the labor force. Although men are still the nation's primary workers, accounting even now for about two-thirds of the labor force, both the interest of women in gainful work and their opportunities have been growing rapidly. Women accounted for 56 per cent of the growth in the adult labor force during the eight years from 1948 to 1956, and they accounted for a still larger fraction—65 per cent—of the growth during the next eight years. Also, as the war babies have been coming of age, young workers have become a larger factor in the labor market. The number of teenagers in the labor force was practically the same in 1956 as in 1948; but they have become much more numerous since then. The increasing role of married women and young people in industry must be kept in mind in interpreting statistics of employment or unemployment. Since women commonly have responsibilities as wives, mothers, or

thirty-five

housekeepers, they tend, on the average, to work fewer hours and less regularly than men. For example, about 48 per cent of the women who worked in 1963 were part-time or intermittent workers, while only 21 per cent of the men can be so classified. And just as family duties make women prone to part-time and intermittent work, so attendance at school has similar consequences for many youngsters. That this factor is of some consequence is evident from the fact that in recent years a little over half of the teenage labor force has consisted of students.

The emergence of a large part-time and intermittent work force is one of the neglected aspects of the changing structure of the American economy. The growth of this part of the labor force has been substantial. Not only are women an increasing part of the nation's work force; it also appears that the proportion among them who seek part-time or intermittent work is tending to become larger. And although the great majority of men continue to be regular full-time workers, the proportion who work part-time or intermittently is also rising—indeed, it is rising faster than among women. Taking the entire working force together, we find that the part-timers and the intermittently employed accounted for 27 per cent of the population with work experience during 1950, for 29 per cent in 1957, and for 31 per cent in 1963. This upward drift reflects, on the side of demand, the rapid growth of trade, clerical tasks, and service occupations. On the supply side, it reflects the spread of public and private pensions, as well as the growing participation of married women and students in gainful employment. Elderly men on a pension can often get along without steady full-time jobs, and not a few of them are driven to part-time or intermittent work by the penalty imposed by our social security system on those whose income exceeds the low statutory maximum.

The changing structure of the labor force has left its mark on both the character and the magnitude of the unemployment problem. Whether unemployment is viewed from the side of efficiency or that of welfare, the unemployment of a student seeking a summer job or the unemployment of a housewife seeking part-time work cannot be readily equated with the unemployment of the family breadwinner who needs a regular full-time job. Furthermore, the increasing participation in the labor force of women, youngsters, students, part-timers, and intermittent workers—these, of course, are overlapping groups —is exerting upward pressure on the unemployment rate.

A new entrant into the labor force rarely finds or takes a job immediately; in other words, he is unemployed for a time. These unavoidable intervals of unemployment tend to be repeated for intermittent workers, among whom part-timers are a large and increasing group. Women, whose role in the economy is growing, are typically less inclined or less able than men to end their unemployment by taking a job in another city. Indeed, they are even less prone to move to another occupation or to another firm within the city of their residence. That, of course, is one reason why the unemployment rate is characteristically higher for women than for men. Also, the unemployment rate for young men and women is consistently much higher in our country than for adults. There are many reasons for this—among them, the limited or utter lack of experience of young people, their low seniority status, and their healthy propensity to test their aptitudes and opportunities by experimenting with different jobs. My point at the moment is merely that youngsters are an increasing part of the nation's total labor force, and that students—who often seek part-time or intermittent work and whose mobility is necessarily very limited—are a large and growing part of the youthful labor force. Although it is difficult to determine the degree to which the various and complex changes in the character of the labor force are tending to influence the unemployment rate, I do not think there can be much doubt that the general effect is upward. One thing we know definitely —persons seeking part-time jobs are an increasing part of unemployment. In 1964 one out of every six unemployed workers was looking for a part-time job, in contrast to one out of thirteen a decade earlier.

Facts such as these deserve more recognition than they usually receive. Certainly, an unemployment rate of four per cent, or for that matter any other fixed figure, is an excessively crude guide to economic policy. It would be an error of judgment, however, to leap to the conclusion that unemployment of the

thirty-seven

magnitude experienced by our nation since 1957 is not a serious matter. Much of our unemployment has been concentrated—and still is—among low income groups, particularly Negroes, whose political voice is now becoming stronger. Unemployment contributes to crime and social tensions, and in recent years it has contributed also to racial strife. Moreover, unemployment tends to be a disrupting influence on people in every station of life, particularly in a society—such as ours—which is accustomed to identifying work with virtue. The fact that growing affluence has made people more selective about jobs, or that some individuals could give up gainful employment without inviting economic hardship, or that many individuals now prefer part-time work, does not mean that jobs have become less vital to personal happiness or individual fulfillment than they were a generation ago. Abundance as well as equality of opportunity is still the great American dream. No matter how we qualify the interpretation of unemployment figures, they do tell us that in recent years our nation has not succeeded as well as it did during the early fifties, or during other periods of prosperity, in enabling men and women—whether young or old, married or single, rich or poor—to fulfill the normal desire of having a job and thus finding usefulness.

The uneven impact of unemployment on people is perhaps its harshest feature. Factory workers and office workers may share the same roof, but the risk of becoming unemployed is much larger for the former than the latter. When a slump in sales or some technological improvement leads a business firm to cut back its work force, the brunt of the adjustment is usually borne by ordinary production hands, especially those with low seniority status, while the supervisory and clerical employees are affected little, if at all. Again, seasonal factors are of little importance in some industries, but a major disturbance in others. Certainly, civil servants or even workers in the steel and automobile industries do not experience protracted periods of seasonal slack such as are common in the construction industry or in food canning or in the garment trades. The business cycle also impinges very unevenly on the lives of working people. When a recession develops and employment declines, the rate of decline is typically much larger for wage-earners than for the self-employed, for blue-collar workers than for white-collar workers, for manufacturing or mining employees than for those engaged in the service trades, and for workers in the durable goods branch of manufacturing than for those in the nondurable branch. These disparities of risk are at the very heart of the unemployment problem. Indeed, if all workers were subject to the same unemployment hazard, in the sense that the unemployment experienced during any year was shared evenly, a five per cent unemployment rate would mean at worst an unpaid—and perhaps unplanned—vacation of about two and a half weeks for everyone. Production would still suffer, but not necessarily the morale or the welfare of people.

The fact that the risk of unemployment has lately become disproportionately high for some major segments of our working population is therefore a troublesome development. Last year the unemployment rate for adult females was a third higher than for adult males. This is the largest such discrepancy in a dozen years. In 1963 the unemployment rate for teenagers was three and a half times that of adult males, and in 1964 this ratio became still larger. There is no precedent for such extreme differentials, at least in the post-war period. The differential between whites and nonwhites has also widened ominously. Since 1955 the unemployment rate for all nonwhites has been rather consistently more than twice that of white workers. In the forties and early fifties, the difference between the two groups was much smaller. In the case of male teenagers, the average ratio of the nonwhite unemployment rate to that for whites was 1.1 for the years between 1950 and 1954, then rose to 1.6 during 1955-59, and reached 1.7 during 1960-64. In the case of female teenagers, the corresponding ratios were 1.5, 2.2, and again 2.2. I do not think that these wider differentials can be explained simply by the persistence of a relatively high rate of unemployment. I find, for example, that the comprehensive unemployment rate was the same in 1950 as in 1964, and yet all these differentials were then appreciably smaller.

The heavy impact of recent unemployment on teenagers, women, and Negroes means, of course, that unemployment has lately become increasingly concentrated among relatively inexperienced and unskilled workers. Available statistics do not enable us to differentiate very precisely between the skilled working population and the unskilled group. However, since experienced and more skilled workers predominate among married men, the unemployment rate for this group gives a clue to what has been happening in the market for skilled labor. So too, although more crudely, does the unemployment rate for adult males or the unemployment rate for insured workers. If we go back to the eighteen-months stretch from January 1956 to June 1957, when the economy was booming and jobs were plentiful nearly everywhere, we find that the unemployment rate averaged 2.4 per cent for married males, 3.4 per cent for adult males, and 3.4 per cent again for insured workers. In the years that followed, the unemployment of these groups became much higher; but by 1964 they began to approximate the 1956-57 boom level, and by the second quarter of this year they were fully back to that level. Meanwhile, the unemployment rate of teenagers, nonwhites, and women has persistently remained above the 1956-57 rates. This year, the gap has narrowed sharply for women, but not for nonwhites or teenagers.

These divergent trends suggest a sort of dual economy, with persistent shortages of skilled labor existing side by side with surpluses of relatively unskilled or inexperienced labor. The first Manpower Report of the President, issued in March 1963, strongly emphasized the prevalence of unemployment, and yet noted a shortage of scientists, teachers, engineers, doctors, nurses, typists, stenographers, automobile and TV mechanics, tailors, and some other types of labor. Since then, the increase of help-wanted advertising indicates that recruitment efforts by employers seeking skilled labor have mounted. And there are also other indications of increased inequality in the distribution of work among our people. During the boom of 1956-57, one out of every 18 or 19 workers engaged in moonlighting, and so it was still in 1963 and in 1964—although the rate of unemployment had become much higher. Meanwhile, overtime work at premium rates, which averaged 2.6 hours per worker in manufacturing during the boom of 1956-57, rose to 2.8 hours in 1963,

3.1 hours in 1964, and 3.4 hours in the first half of this year. In view of the extensiveness of overtime, it need surprise no one that part-time idleness—that is, the extent to which individuals seeking full-time work find themselves on part-time schedules—has been running lower this year and last than it did during the boom of 1956-57. Clearly, serious shortages in some major sectors of the labor market have been existing side by side with high unemployment, much of it of a long-term character, in other sectors.

In our dynamic economy, shortages in some parts of the labor market frequently accompany surpluses elsewhere without becoming a matter of national concern. They are apt to become that, however, when the correction of the disequilibrium proceeds slowly; that is, when geographic pockets of chronic depression emerge or when persistently high unemployment develops in some major industries or occupations or other social groups. Two schools of thought on the unemployment problem have made their voice heard in recent years. According to the expansionists, whose views have dominated public policy in recent years, the fundamental cause of our relatively high rate of unemployment is a deficiency of aggregate demand. The structuralist school, on the other hand, claims that the fundamental cause is the intensified tempo of economic change, which has created more jobs than can be filled in some occupations and communities while substantial unemployment exists or is being created in others. In principle, these differences of diagnosis could be settled by comparing the size and composition of unemployment with the number and composition of vacant jobs. Unhappily, despite the general excellence of our statistical system, even rough statistics of job vacancies are unavailable on a nation-wide basis. The protagonists of the two schools have therefore had to rely on indirect and circumstantial evidence.

In the early stages of the debate, the expansionists tended to minimize the importance of structural changes. They took their stand on the theoretical ground that once aggregate demand increased sufficiently, the groups that have been suffering from abnormally high rates of unemployment would find their position dramatically improved. By and large, the structuralists conceded the theory. They insisted, however, that the improvement would come much too slowly, that it would involve the nation in inflation, and that the problem of unemployment could be solved without this heavy cost by concentrating on policies for better matching of jobs and workers. As the discussion proceeded, the gap between the two schools narrowed. The evidence amassed by the structuralists gradually led the expansionists to give greater weight to geographic, occupational, industrial, and other imbalances in the labor market. Also, since the new labor market policies proposed by the structuralists often required additions to governmental expenditure, they were to that extent welcomed by the expansionists. The expansionist school has persisted, however, in denying that structural factors are a greater cause of the unemployment of the past few years than they were in earlier times.

As far as I can judge, the expansionist theory is sounder in what it claims than in what it denies. In view of the fact that our nation experienced a recession in 1957-58, that the recovery which followed was incomplete, that another recession occurred in 1960-61, and that a good part of 1962 was marked by sluggishness, there can be little doubt that a deficiency of aggregate demand was a major cause of unemployment during much of the period since 1957. However, there are cogent grounds for believing that if the pressure of aggregate demand had remained at the boom level of 1956-57, the unemployment rate would still have been higher in recent years than it was then. In addition to the factors I have already noted, statistics on productivity suggest that the displacement of labor through technological and other improvements in industry has proceeded somewhat faster during the past few years than it did during the late fifties. To the extent that this has occurred, it has complicated the adjustment of the supply of labor to the changing requirements of employers. At any rate, with a part-time and intermittent work force growing, with a tendency toward voluntary unemployment increasing, with the employment opportunities of the unskilled declining, and with inequality in the distribution of work increasing, it appears that our economy has been changing in ways that make it harder to achieve full employment merely by stimulating aggregate demand. If this generalization is valid, as I am increasingly inclined to believe, it would be wise to devote much more attention than we are giving to policies for facilitating the mutual adjustment of supply and demand in the labor market.

Fortunately, recognition of this need is increasing. While the dominant emphasis of economic policy in the past few years has been on the expansion of aggregate demand, numerous programs have also been initiated to improve the functioning of the labor market. These programs run the gamut from training people for available jobs to helping workers relocate where the jobs are or bringing new jobs to depressed areas. I cannot stop to examine or evaluate these programs. Surely, some suffer from being spread too thinly, and others are handicapped by overlapping authority or conflicting provisions. But what is chiefly important, the new activities being directed to the training or retraining of unemployed or poorly adjusted workers seem to be very promising. At first, these activities were focused exclusively on vocational skills, but they are now being broadened—I think wisely—to include also instruction in the rudiments of language, arithmetic, and personal conduct. These new educational efforts are still being conducted on a small scale, and it would be desirable to expand them as experience is gained and as the needed teaching and counseling staffs become available. We must not overlook, however, the lesson to be drawn from earlier experience with vocational education, namely, that constant vigilance is needed to assure that the teaching and counseling are realistically geared to the changing job requirements of employers. In 1918, when federal concern with vocational education started, less than 30 per cent of those enrolled in federally aided vocational classes received instruction in home economics or agriculture. Incredible though it may seem, this proportion had grown by 1963 to over 60 per cent, while technical education languished.

Our governmental authorities recognize that the success of the new training programs will depend heavily on the effectiveness of the federal-state employment service. However, the measures that have thus far been taken to invigorate this branch of the governmental apparatus are quite insufficient. Modern high-speed electronic computers and telecommunication have opened up exciting opportunities that the employment service should by now be exploiting. With their aid, it should be possible for an unemployed person to walk into a local employment office, express his need or preference for work, and be referred in a matter of hours, if not minutes, to a list of plausible jobs in his own community, or—if none are available there—to jobs in more distant places. Employers seeking to fill vacancies could be similarly served. If the employment service took full advantage of modern technology and began to function in this manner, our labor market—or rather that part of it being served by the public employment system—would become so organized that supply and demand could, in principle, be matched almost instantly. Some reduction of the level of unemployment, perhaps a very substantial reduction, is virtually bound to be achieved through such a reform. The results, of course, would be all the better if some practical way could be devised of coordinating the activities of public and private employment offices.

The effectiveness of the new training programs in reducing unemployment will depend also on how speedily and how accurately the authorities can detect shifts in occupational and industrial trends. Although good statistics are not enough to make good forecasts, they are an indispensable tool to the analyst and forecaster. Statistics on unemployment have already proved very helpful in the analysis of labor market trends, but there is as much need for statistics on job vacancies as for statistics on unemployment. Recent research and experiments have demonstrated that useful statistics on job vacancies can be collected on a current basis, and the Department of Labor has therefore sought an appropriation for this purpose. In view of the need for job vacancy statistics on the part of administrators of the new training programs as well as local school authorities, vocational counselors, personnel officers, and practical economists concerned with labor market problems, I have no doubt that the Congress will in time provide the necessary funds; but it would be wise to take early steps to supply this vital missing link in our system of economic intelligence.

Besides devoting energy to new labor market programs, it is desirable to reappraise older governmental programs that influence the efficiency of the labor market. One of these is the social security system which has strengthened our economy and brought blessings to many millions, but which has also had some unhappy side effects. Whatever may be said of present eligibility requirements for unemployment insurance, they have not stiffened sufficiently to cope with the increasing trend toward part-time and intermittent work. Too many individuals are tempted to work for a short time, then leave and draw unemployment insurance. Also, too many employers manage to attach workers to their establishments by a combination of subnormal wages and the assurance of unemployment benefits during protracted periods of seasonal slack. Of course, the employees of such subsidized firms often become unemployed only in a technical sense. The same is true of workers who have just retired on a pension and yet draw unemployment insurance. To the extent that these conditions prevail, they cry out for remedy. If such abuses were stopped or substantially reduced, our actual as well as statistical unemployment would be somewhat lower, and there would be the added advantage that public policy could then look more favorably on the liberalization of benefits for the great mass of the unemployed who are truly willing and seeking to work.

More important still, there is a need to improve our understanding of the effects of minimum wage laws on the workings of the labor market. I have already noted the great influx of women and teenagers into the labor force in recent years. This major development in the market for relatively unskilled labor has been reinforced, on the supply side, by migration of both whites and Negroes from farms to the cities. Meanwhile, many employers have been finding ways of economizing on costs by substituting machinery or other automatic devices for unskilled or semiskilled labor. In these circumstances, in order to perform the function of bringing the demand for labor and its supply into mutual adjustment, the price of unskilled labor should have declined in recent years relative to the price of skilled labor.

forty-five

As far as I have been able to learn from the meager accessible data, this did not happen. For example, records for the construction industry show an increase in average hourly wages of 40 per cent between 1956 and 1964 for skilled labor and 50 per cent for common labor. During the same period, the average hourly wage rose 36 per cent for skilled maintenance workers in manufacturing plants, and the increase was the same for unskilled workers. Again during this period, the minimum union wage rose 41 per cent for drivers engaged in local trucking and 43 per cent for their helpers. Systematic data for office employees go back only to 1958. Here we find that the average wage of office boys has risen more since 1958 than that of accounting clerks, and that the average wage of file clerks has risen more than that of any other group of female office workers. These comparisons, it should be noted, are useful only in judging the skilled-unskilled differential of a particular industry or group. They cannot be used to compare industries, since the samples differ and so too does the treatment of fringe benefits.

If the wage trends that I have cited are at all representative, it appears that the skilled-unskilled wage differential has lately been out of equilibrium; in other words, unskilled labor has been relatively overpriced. One reason for this development is the tendency of trade unions to press for uniform or even narrower wage differentials between skilled and unskilled work. Another and more powerful reason is the minimum wage legislation of our federal government. During the post-war period, the minimum wage per hour has been raised four times, first in January 1950 when it went up from forty to seventy-five cents, next in March 1956 when it rose to a dollar, then in September 1961 to a dollar and fifteen cents, and in September 1963 to a dollar and a quarter. Each time the minimum was raised, it was set at approximately half of the average manufacturing wage. However, the statutory minimum was only 29 per cent of average hourly earnings in manufacturing just before the increase of 1950, while the corresponding figure reached 40 per cent just before the increase of the minimum in 1956, 43 per cent before the increase in 1961, and 47 per cent before the increase in 1963. There has thus been a strong upward drift across the years in the actual ratio of the minimum wage to the average wage. This drift is most simply indicated by the fact that the minimum wage rose 67 per cent between early 1956 and 1964, while average hourly earnings in manufacturing rose 34 per cent. Meanwhile, the federal minimum has become effective over a greater range of industry, and many states have likewise raised or expanded the coverage of their minimum wages.

When the statutory minimum wage rises, the effects spread out. In the first place, forces are set in motion to restore previous differentials, so that there is a tendency for the entire lower end of the wage structure to be lifted. Secondly, the higher minimum has an influence on prevailing attitudes and opinion. Not a few uncovered workers are apt to feel that they too are entitled to a higher minimum and that nothing else would be just. This sentiment is often shared by others, including businessmen in the community, so that even some reluctant employers give way. However, the mere raising of the statutory minimum does nothing of itself to improve the productivity of workers, and it therefore also does nothing to enhance their worth to employers. In a large and complex economy such as ours, there is always some range of substitution, depending on relative costs, between skilled and unskilled workers or between labor and machinery of this or that degree of automaticity. The broad result of the substantial increase of the minimum wage in recent years has therefore been a curtailment of job opportunities for the less skilled workers. With unskilled labor being overpriced, employers have been using relatively more capital or skilled labor and relatively less unskilled labor. Large firms have frequently made this adjustment in the course of expanding their operations, while many small businesses that previously managed with a helper or two have learned to get along with just one or without any.

These broad observations are borne out by statistical evidence. During the post-war period, the ratio of the unemployment rate of teenagers to that of male adults was invariably higher during the six months following an increase of the minimum wage than it was in the preceding half year. The ratio of the unemployment rate of female adults to that of male adults has behaved similarly. Of course, the unemployment of teen-agers and women depends on a variety of factors—certainly on business conditions as well as on the minimum wage. I have tried to allow for this in a more refined analysis. It appears, whether we consider the unemployment rate of teenagers or that of women, that its primary determinants are, first, the general state of the economy as indicated by the unemployment rate of adult males, second, the ratio of the minimum wage to the average wage in manufacturing. The influence of the wage ratio turns out to be particularly strong in the case of nonwhite teenagers. According to my equation, it appears that in the absence of any change in the general state of the economy, another increase of twenty-five cents in the minimum wage would be likely to raise the unemployment rate of nonwhite teenagers by as much as eight percentage points. This, I need hardly say, is a very disturbing estimate. However, the same equation also indicates that a reduction of the ratio of the mini-mum wage to the average wage tends to lower the unemploy-ment rate. In other words, the slow reduction of this ratio since 1963, when the minimum wage was last set, has contributed somewhat to the improvement that has recently taken place in the teenage unemployment rate. Of course, the effort made during the past few months to enroll teenagers in various train-ing programs has also contributed modestly to this result.

The subject of minimum wages is so surrounded by human emotion and political commitment that sensible reform may prove extremely difficult in the near future. Compassionate concern for the poor does credit to our age, and yet the pro-grams to which it gives rise can be effective only to the degree that they meet the test of economic soundness. The surest way to improve the income of poor people is to help them become more productive, and that is why the new training programs undertaken by the government deserve encouragement. How-ever, some unfortunate people are so handicapped that they cannot become more productive. Hence, there is also some-thing to be said for a society that would assure a minimum income for every family. Legislation of a minimum hourly wage does no such thing. It helps some of the poor and harms others

—often those who need help most. In view of our nation's newly aroused interest in the problem of poverty, economists can no longer ignore, as they virtually have, the minimum wage. Young people, both white and Negro, will soon be entering the labor force in much larger numbers, and it would be unfortunate if sentimental attachment to the minimum wage were allowed to continue to obstruct their opportunity to get jobs. If nothing else can be done, it would prove helpful to make special provision for teenagers by lowering for the next two or three years the minimum that is applicable to them. A lower minimum wage would enable more youngsters to find jobs, and it would also give employers more incentive to train them.

Beyond the questions of policy that I have discussed, there is a great need for more vigorous research on labor market problems. The rate of unemployment today is appreciably lower than it was a year or two ago, and it may before long reach four per cent—a level that economists often associate with "full employment." That condition, however, would still mean extensive unemployment for some significant parts of the working population. Partly for this reason, and partly also because the labor force will probably rise more rapidly in the years ahead, we should prepare for the future by improving our basic knowledge. According to a study by the Bureau of Labor Statistics, seasonal variations in industry and trade account for at least 20 per cent of total unemployment in a good business year. This major source of unemployment is not receiving the attention it deserves. The growth of overtime is another subject that calls for research. While scarcity of skilled labor may well be the principal cause of this development, other causes have been suggested. One is the steady expansion of fringe benefits, the cost of which to a business firm tends to vary with the number of men employed rather than with the number of manhours worked. Another is that employers are finding that disputes about work rules are fewer when they resort to overtime than when they rearrange jobs in the process of adding to their work force. Still another factor is that some large employers seek to regularize the number of jobs in order to maintain good community relations, and this necessarily means more overtime when sales are brisk. These and other suggested causes of the growth of overtime need to be thoroughly investigated and a more constructive solution sought than the proposal to raise the premium rates on overtime—a proposal that would inevitably raise costs of production and, in the end, perhaps add to unemployment instead of relieving it. Still another highly important subject for research revolves around the need for business planning of technological improvements or of shifts in plant location so as to ease the problem of adjustment for the employees.

Let me say, finally, that in urging better labor market policies, I have assumed that the managers of national prosperity will seek to maintain aggregate demand at a high level. I have not stressed this need, because at present there is little danger that the state of demand will suffer from neglect. The danger is rather that philosophical commitment to the theory of deficiency in aggregate demand has now become so strong that it will lead us to seek through a liberal monetary and fiscal policy what can be achieved at lesser cost, and with more lasting effect, by attending to the structural causes of unemployment.

November 2, 1965

III. Pathways to stable prosperity

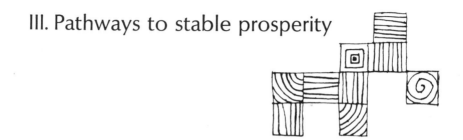

III. Pathways to stable prosperity

A great, if not the greatest, economic achievement of the post-war period is the moderation of the business cycle in our nation and in others that practice free enterprise on an extensive scale. The ability of Western capitalism, and especially of the American economy, to generate expansion, improve productivity, widen opportunity, and diffuse well being had been amply demonstrated during the preceding century. Our economic growth, however, came in spurts, each great leap forward being followed by a slump in production, employment, and profits. The contractions in economic activity usually proved much smaller than the expansions that preceded them, and a few—such as the declines of 1887-88 and 1926-27—were merely pauses in the growth of the domestic economy. There were, however, other declines, such as those of the 1870's and 1890's, which were both protracted and severe, while the depression of the 1930's became a world-wide upheaval of catastrophic proportions. The Marxian prophecy that the economic crises of capitalism would become increasingly severe and eventually lead to a collapse of the capitalist order did not seem remote or far-fetched in 1932.

The search for ways of preventing or moderating business cycles started long before the Great Depression, but it became much more intense as a result of that catastrophe. In our country, thoughtful citizens at first concentrated on ways of dealing with financial crises. The Federal Reserve Act, which became law under the shadow of the crisis of 1907, sought to deal with this problem by requiring the pooling of bank reserves. Later, in response to the violent movements of the price level between 1914 and 1921, the authorities of the newly organized Federal Reserve System sought to moderate the movements of credit in the hope that price and business fluctuations would be tamed in the process. In the course of these efforts, they developed the technique of open-market operations, which has proved a highly useful tool in economic stabilization. But the Federal Reserve System could not deal adequately with the boisterous speculation in common stocks, real estate, and foreign bonds that developed during the twenties. Nor could it later prevent

fifty-three

massive bank failures or runs on banks. Nor were its powers sufficient to deal with the recurring problem of unemployment even under less trying circumstances than developed during the Great Depression.

The urgent need to strengthen defenses against the business cycle prompted many reforms during the thirties, among them development of the long-term amortized mortgage, the regulation of stock exchanges, the insurance of mortgages, the insurance of savings and loan accounts, and—more important still—the insurance of bank deposits. But more basic than these financial innovations, or the other measures of policy that were adopted to lay the groundwork for economic recovery, was the change that occurred in economic and political attitudes. The traditional belief that it was best to leave business storms to blow themselves out lost its grip on men's minds as the depression stretched out. In increasing numbers citizens in all walks of life joined the reformers in urging that mass unemployment was intolerable in a growing urban society and that the federal government must assume a larger and more definite responsibility for promoting economic conditions that would afford employment opportunities for all those able, willing, and seeking to work. The new philosophy gained support during the forties, when many thousands of our finest youth lost their lives on the battlefield but unemployment practically vanished once aggregate demand for goods and services grew sufficiently. Intelligent men reasoned that if the government can eliminate unemployment in a time of war, it should also seek to approximate this result—preferably by stimulating private activity but if need be by its own spending—in a time of peace. This new philosophy of intervention was articulated by Congress in the Employment Act of 1946, which expressed what had by then become a national consensus.

In recent decades, therefore, the business cycle has no longer run a free course. Taking seriously its new responsibility, the federal government has used extensively its monetary, fiscal, and regulatory powers to promote a stable prosperity. Its contracyclical efforts have not always been well-timed or appropriate to the need, but by and large they have proved constructive.

So too, on their more limited plane, have the efforts of the business community to control inventories. Meanwhile, a favorable conjuncture of structural changes in the economy, many of which were entirely unconnected with planning for stability, has facilitated the task of the managers of national prosperity.

The employment structure of our country has become transformed in recent decades, and the trend has been preponderantly in a stabilizing direction. Manufacturing, mining, construction work, freight transportation—these are the cyclically volatile industries; but their relative importance as providers of jobs has for some years been declining, while that of the more stable service industries has been increasing. In addition, the proportion of people who work as managers, engineers, scientists, accountants, secretaries, salesmen, or are otherwise engaged in occupations that have something of an overhead character has been rising rapidly, while the proportion of "blue collar" workers—whose jobs are typically much less steady—has been falling. These changes in the industrial and occupational structure have served to blunt the impact of cyclical declines of industrial production on the lives of working people.

Other developments in our economy have helped to stabilize private incomes by creating a buffer between the fluctuations of production and the flow of income to individuals. During each of the recessions of the post-war period, the government has offset automatically and to a significant degree the decline in the flow of income from production, first, by collecting much less in taxes from corporations and individuals, second, by increasing unemployment insurance and other social security payments. Corporations, in turn, have reacted to the decline in their profits by reducing their savings rather than the flow of dividends or pensions to individuals. Such automatic stabilizers have long been a feature of the American economy, but they have become much more powerful in our generation as a result of the vast expansion of government, the increased role of the income tax in public revenues, the shift of income tax collection to a pay-as-you-go basis, the growth of unemployment insurance and other programs of social security, the growing frequency and scale of private pensions, the spread of business

fifty-five

corporations, and their increasing pursuit of stable dividend policies.

In short, several major developments—the more active role of government in promoting stable prosperity, more efficient control of inventories by the business community, and structural changes in the economy—have combined to moderate the business cycle. More than twenty-five years have already elapsed since we last had a severe economic decline. Over thirty years have elapsed since we last experienced a financial panic. Since 1937 we have had six recessions, the longest of which lasted only 13 months. Since 1945 we have experienced five recessions, but even the severest of these was less intense than the average pre-war decline. This sequence of relatively mild and brief contractions marks a break with the long past. Moreover, while contractions have become shorter and milder, expansions have tended to become longer. The duration of the four expansions between 1945 and 1960 averaged 36 months, in contrast to an average duration of 26 months for the ten expansions from 1900 to 1937. And the current expansion, which has already lasted longer than any of its peacetime predecessors of which we have a definite record, is still running strong.

In view of this record of achievement, the business cycle has lost much of its terror. Most businessmen, government officials, trade union leaders, and other influential citizens now take it for granted that the course of the economy will be shaped in large part by governmental policy and that the more serious mistakes of the past can and will be avoided. Certainly, no administration nowadays would tolerate destruction of one-third of the nation's money supply during a period of declining economic activity. Yet that is precisely what our government permitted to happen between the fall of 1929 and the spring of 1933. Nor is any administration soon likely to raise taxes all around at a time of heavy unemployment, which is what the Congress kept ordering from 1932 to 1936. We have learned to avoid such blunders of policy, and we have become more mindful of the need to pursue economic objectives in ways that take account of the state of confidence.

Recent progress in moderating the business cycle has stirred the wholesome hope that we may do still better in the future. Unhappily, it has also given rise to the view, which is spreading among businessmen as well as intellectuals, that the business cycle has already been mastered. This view has been encouraged by the durability of the current economic expansion, by the role of the government in prolonging it, and especially by the success of the recent tax reductions which were undertaken to reinforce expansion rather than to counteract any recession. On all sides we hear that a "new economics" has been born, that the federal government is now able, by adjusting taxes or its own rate of spending, to keep the aggregate demand for goods and services closely adjusted to what our economy can produce at full employment, and that the government has finally resolved to manage prosperity in this fashion.

The "new economics," or the new fiscal theory which is its essence, undoubtedly provides a useful framework for economic thinking about some of the problems that surround our national prosperity. It would be unwise, however, to permit this theory or any other to lull us into the belief that prosperity is assured by the government. The new fiscal theory might help to reduce mistakes in governmental policy, but it surely cannot prevent mistakes.

Before the new theory can be applied, forecasts must be made of the nation's capacity to produce and of what actual production would be in the absence of fresh governmental actions. Economic forecasting, however, is still a rudimentary art. Indeed, even our knowledge of the present is quite imperfect, as the revised estimates of national income that the Department of Commerce published earlier this year have helped to remind us. Experience indicates that the best of experts not infrequently make serious mistakes when they attempt to predict the gross national product more than six months ahead. Needless to say, the forecasts required by the new fiscal theory are vastly more difficult. It is also well to bear in mind that the new theory disregards the structure, as distinguished from the level, of both taxes and expenditures, and that it equates—except for a technical factor involving savings—the stimulative power of tax reduction to that of increased governmental spending. Since the theory proceeds on a highly abstract plane, as theories generally do, it cannot of itself provide much practical guidance on ways of nourishing the main source of our national prosperity—which is still, as it has always been, the hopefulness, skill, and energy of the American people.

Moreover, fiscal policy does not encompass all of governmental action. Important though fiscal policy is, it must still be fitted in with other matters of large governmental concern—that is, policies involving gold, the labor market, corporate mergers, education, defense, foreign trade, and so on. These policies too have their influence on the state of confidence and prosperity. Indeed, the effectiveness of a particular fiscal policy will always depend on what other policies have been recently pursued or are currently being pursued. An expansionist fiscal policy, for example, may come to naught if credit is simultaneously being restricted. Or to give a historical example, the proposal that President Roosevelt made in early 1937 to enlarge the membership of the Supreme Court would have caused little stir outside of legal and academic circles had it been made by President Hoover in early 1929. As it was, this proposal followed a mass of legislation that deeply disturbed the business community, and it came at a time when a wave of sit-down strikes posed a threat to property rights. In these circumstances, it was widely feared that the Supreme Court proposal was a step toward abridgment of constitutional safeguards of private property. I doubt if any fiscal policy that was plausible at the time could have prevented the collapse that occurred in business confidence and investment.

As these remarks suggest, it is unrealistic to expect the "new economics" to protect government officials from making mistakes in their efforts to manage prosperity. In fact, by helping to bend governmental policy toward inflation, the new fiscal theory will at times promote mistakes, just as the older theory of balanced budgets did by bending governmental policy at times toward deflation. To be sure, the new theory requires that the government should reduce spending or increase taxes, if aggregate demand keeps growing faster than productive capacity once full employment has been achieved. In actual life, however, inflationary pressures do not wait until this point is reached. They usually emerge much earlier—that is, when the presence of a gap between productive capacity and actual production still requires, according to the theory, an expansionist fiscal policy. The theoretical system of the "new economics" cannot deal with this early type of inflation because it falls outside the system. Hence, the adherents of the theory are forced to resort to improvisation—which may be guidelines for wages and prices today, and something else tomorrow. The steel price episode of April 1962 should suffice to remind us that here too is a source of possible misadventures.

I need not labor further the point that the "new economics" provides no assurance of continuing prosperity. Nor does the history of our times, to say nothing of the long past, provide any such assurance. What history discloses is a succession of business cycles no two of which have ever been alike. The business cycle of experience is a highly variable phenomenon. If the current expansion in economic activity has been exceptionally long, it has also been less vigorous than some of its predecessors. Long though the current expansion has been, another two years will need to elapse before it can match the one that spanned World War II. Protracted expansions have been fairly common abroad, but recessions have nevertheless occurred. Japan is now in the throes of a recession while Italy is recovering from one. And in our own country, the economy is no longer displaying the balance that characterized the earlier stages of expansion. Signs of strain, such as normally occur during the upswing of the business cycle, have been multiplying, and it is only prudent to recognize them.

One of our great economic assets in the past few years has been the comparative absence of an inflationary psychology. With our wholesale price level steady, while other industrial nations were practicing inflation, we were able to increase our export surplus and thereby check the deterioration in the balance of payments. We were also able to avoid inventory speculation, overbuilding of industrial facilities, or a cost-price squeeze in critical manufacturing industries. Now, however, with economic exuberance quickening, the precious asset of general price stability may be going to waste. Of late, consumers have not only been spending liberally their rising incomes, but also borrowing at an increasing rate. Business firms have been borrowing heavily to enlarge their capital expenditures, which are growing at a pace that is adding to inflationary pressures and threatening a later imbalance between industrial capacity and production. State and local governments too have been sharing in the mood of prosperity by increasing both their spending and their debts. For a while, in order to facilitate Congressional acceptance of a massive tax reduction, the federal government stabilized its spending. That period lasted about eighteen months and is already at an end. A new upsurge of federal spending has gotten under way, with welfare and other civilian programs expanding rapidly at the very time that the war in Vietnam is becoming a larger burden on our material and financial resources. Under the circumstances, cost and price pressures are increasing. An inflationary psychology is again becoming a force in the market place, and this may lead to economic trouble.

To be sure, in view of the substantial progress toward economic stability that our nation has made in this generation, it would be reasonable to assume that future recessions will be milder on the average than they were before the 1940's. But if we assume more than that, our hopes may mislead our practical judgment. The forces that generate business cycles are still with us. Economic trends can shift with little or no notice. The structure of our economy, which has been changing on balance in a stabilizing direction, need not continue to do that. Military expenditures, for example, which necessarily depend on international developments, could become a larger source of instability. Our economy is not insulated against political or financial shocks from abroad. The machinery of governmental policy-making sometimes moves slowly, and the policies themselves may be inadequate or inappropriate. Rather than cling to delusions about perpetual prosperity, let us do what we can as a people, first, to prevent overheating of the economy in the immediate future, second, to strengthen our defenses against future recessions.

Whatever may have been the case a year or two ago, it should be clear from the more recent behavior of wages and prices that the federal government cannot continue pursuing policies that release powerful expansionist forces and yet trust that its guideposts for prices and wages will prevent inflation. Continuance of governmental reliance on the guideposts merely postpones corrective measures. Worse still, it may excite public clamor for direct price and wage controls—a grim expedient that would indeed suppress inflation for a time, but at the cost of impairing efficiency as well as crushing economic freedom. The wise course is to check gradually the rate of expansion of credit and to check more sharply, in view of rapidly rising military costs, the growth of federal spending on civilian programs. These steps are bound to be difficult politically; but if they are postponed, there is a danger that they will come too late or need to be blunt.

A less liberal monetary and fiscal policy is now advisable not only in the interests of the domestic economy, but also for reasons connected with our international dealings. One of the factors that has contributed significantly to the chronic deficit in our balance of payments is the rapid expansion of credit and the money supply in recent years. During the decade ending in 1960, bank credit—that is, total loans and investments of commercial banks—grew by seven billion dollars per year on the average. Since then, the annual increases have moved from 15 to 18 to 21 billion dollars; and this year's increase—if the pace during the first nine months is maintained—will reach 25 billion. At least until this spring, the commercial banks were so amply equipped with reserves supplied by the monetary authorities that they found themselves hunting for customers abroad as well as at home. Undoubtedly, both the banks and other investors were frequently tempted also by the higher interest rates that can be earned in other countries. Many corporations, in turn, found it advantageous to transfer domestic funds to finance their direct investments abroad. Foreign corporations and governments, in their turn, found our financial market attractive for floating new capital issues. Thus, easy credit conditions fostered a substantial and continuing outflow of private funds.

sixty-one

The government was reluctant to tighten the credit market in view of the persistence of unemployment, although it did recognize the need of somewhat higher short-term interest rates. That mild response did not suffice to stem the outflow of capital. As the outflow persisted, the government sought to deal with the balance of payments problem by resorting to special devices for controlling capital movements. First, the interest equalization tax—which is essentially a protective tariff on the import of securities—was adopted. Later, when the outflow of capital swelled along other channels, the government persuaded the larger banks and business corporations to restrict their foreign loans and investments. This "voluntary program," which was put into effect last March, is of course another barrier to the free movement of capital and trade that our nation has traditionally promoted, both in our own long-run interest and that of the world economy. Thus far the program for restricting foreign loans and investments, or at least that part of it involving bank credits and the placement of corporate funds abroad, has worked quite well.

It is doubtful, however, whether we have as yet achieved more than a temporary improvement in the balance of payments. The benefits from the voluntary program are likely to diminish gradually, as business corporations and other investors become less tolerant of its restraints and inevitable inequities. Meanwhile, the war in Vietnam is adding to the drain of military expenditures abroad. More serious still, our export surplus appears to be diminishing. On the one hand, imports are continuing to rise briskly in response to the expansion of the domestic economy. Exports, on the other hand, have become sluggish because the growth of the world economy has slowed down. This, in turn, is due in good part to the determined effort that most nations in Western Europe have recently been making to restrain the inflationary pressures under which their economies have been laboring. If our wholesale prices should rise appreciably in the next year or so, while other nations succeed in stabilizing their price level, the competitive power of American producers would be reduced, and this would reinforce the restrictive effect on our exports of the slowing down in the growth of the world economy.

The consequences of a renewed deterioration in our balance of payments can be very serious. For many years foreign central banks helped to finance our balance-of-payments deficits by making short-term investments here. This they are now less willing to do, as the loss of a billion and a half dollars of our gold since January eloquently testifies. An early and definite end to deficits in our balance of payments has thus become essential to external confidence in the dollar. Unless that is maintained, our capacity for political leadership among the nations of the world will be weakened and the international monetary system may suffer critical damage.

Of course, a shift to a less liberal monetary and fiscal policy also involves risks. There is always a chance that the shift will be handled clumsily and a recession brought on in the process. Moreover, we still have too much unemployment, and the government is rightly committed to a policy of reducing it. But this objective can be pursued by dealing more vigorously with the structural causes of unemployment, rather than continuing to press expansion with monetary and fiscal tools. The theory that aggregate demand is still deficient has lost much of the plausibility that it had during earlier stages of our economic expansion. After all, the aggregate demand for labor includes the unfilled jobs as well as those that are being manned, just as the aggregate supply of labor includes the unemployed workers as well as those who have jobs. In pursuing a full employment policy, the managers of prosperity have developed the habit of comparing actual production with fragile estimates of potential output. These comparisons may mislead us. The vital relationship is between the aggregate demand for labor and the aggregate supply of labor—or, what comes to the same thing, between the number of vacant jobs and the number of the unemployed. Unfortunately, since our government has not yet taken the trouble to gather the facts, we cannot be certain what the relationship is currently between job vacancies and unemployment. We do know, however, from records on help-wanted advertising and of jobs registered with public employment offices, that job vacancies have of late been increasing rapidly, so that more

sixty-three

attention to labor market policies can surely prove effective in reducing unemployment.

It is important, moreover, to lay plans so that a policy of full employment may be pursued in the future with less danger of inflation. For this purpose, carefully compiled and comprehensive statistics on job vacancies are essential. When the amount of unemployment is larger than the number of job vacancies at existing wages, the aggregate demand for labor is clearly insufficient to provide employment for everyone who is able, willing, and seeking to work. At such a time, a deficiency of aggregate demand exists, and a governmental policy that relies on monetary and fiscal devices to expand demand is, in principle, suited to the nation's needs. On the other hand, when the number of vacant jobs is equal to or larger than the number of the unemployed, there is no deficiency of aggregate demand. A government that is seriously concerned about inflation will not seek to expand aggregate demand at such a time, but will instead concentrate its efforts on securing better matching of the men and women who seek work with the jobs that need to be filled. By equipping ourselves in the future with the information needed to determine whether, when, or to what degree aggregate demand is deficient, we should be able to pursue the objective of full employment with less danger of causing serious inflation.

In considering the future, it is also important to keep in mind, as President Johnson wisely observed in his Economic Report of last January, that "a time of prosperity with no recession in sight is the time to plan our defenses against future dips in business activity." Re-establishment of equilibrium in the balance of payments, or better still the achievement of a moderate surplus for a year or two, would contribute to this objective. In the first place, it would give more room for manoeuvre to our monetary authorities, which they will need in the event of recession. Second, a stronger balance of payments, provided we achieve it with a minimum of protectionist devices, would enable our country to exercise more effective leadership in reforming the international monetary system to facilitate the future growth of the world economy on which our own fortunes heavily depend.

We also need to strengthen the unemployment insurance

system, which aids the economy by maintaining the flow of income to individuals at the very times when income derived from production is depressed. By extending coverage to some of the millions who are still denied this protection, a larger part of the loss during recessions can be offset. This objective will be further served by providing for a more or less automatic extension of benefits during periods of abnormally large unemployment. In 1958 and again in 1961, when unemployment rose on account of the recession in business activity, the Congress passed legislation to extend temporarily the duration of benefits. In each instance, however, the supplementary benefits became available only after recovery started. We can be quite sure that the Congress will not sit idly by when the next recession strikes. But unless the Congress acts in the near future, there is a risk that the supplementary benefits will once again come too late to serve as an effective brake on the forces of recession.

The case for stand-by legislation that would provide for extended duration of unemployment insurance at a fairly early stage of recessions is a compelling one. However, to derive maximum practical benefit from this reform, other changes in the unemployment insurance system are also required. If we permit a larger flow of benefit payments to the unemployed but do nothing else, more marginal workers will be tempted to join the labor force and some of the unemployed will tend to proceed more leisurely in searching for new jobs, thus nullifying, at least in part, the stabilizing effects of the liberalized unemployment benefits. To avoid such frustrations, the liberalization of unemployment insurance needs to be accompanied by stiffer eligibility requirements, so that seasonal and intermittent workers, who are already a heavy drain on the insurance system, may largely be kept out. The administration of insurance benefits also needs to be stiffened, so that anyone who loses his job because of misconduct, or who quits without good cause, or who refuses to take a suitable job, is in fact—not merely nominally, as is now the case in numerous localities—excluded from benefits.

In laying plans for better management of prosperity in the future, it would also be desirable to seek legislation permitting fairly prompt tax reduction if the economy needed stimulation. To achieve this objective, economists have frequently proposed that the Congress pass stand-by legislation that would empower the President to put into effect a temporary reduction of the personal income tax, within limits specified by statute, once a recession started or threatened. In 1962 President Kennedy actually recommended such a law. He knew, of course, that the Congress is accustomed to guarding jealously its power over the public purse and that delegation of any significant part of its taxing power to the President was out of the question for the present. He hoped, however, that discussion would be stimulated and that some future Congress would look more favorably on the proposal. As events turned out, the Congress did not even consider the proposal. In view of this experience, and yet feeling a need for stronger anti-recession planning, President Johnson cautiously suggested in this year's Economic Report that "the Congress could reinforce confidence that jobs and markets will be sustained by insuring that its procedures will permit rapid action on temporary income tax cuts if recession threatens." However, the President did not indicate what the procedures might be or whether the temporary tax reduction should be confined to the personal income tax.

This subject is shot through with political as well as economic difficulties, and my own views on it have undergone a change over the years. I continue to see a need for fairly prompt tax reduction in the event of a recession and also for some flexibility at other stages of the business cycle. I think, however, that this need should be fitted, as far as possible, into a tax policy that is primarily designed to stimulate economic growth. Our present tax system is so constituted that it tends to cushion an economic decline automatically—which is a good thing; but our tax system also tends to check economic expansion automatically—and this is often undesirable. If temporary changes in income tax rates were superimposed on the present tax system, they would accentuate those tendencies. That is to say, a temporary tax reduction at a time of recession would reinforce the automatic cushioning effect of lower tax liabilities. Later, however, when the economy is again advancing, the restoration of tax rates to their original level would add to the already rising tax liabilities and thus reinforce the automatic drag of the tax system on the process of expansion. These tendencies are now better understood than they were only a few years ago. It is doubtful, therefore, whether a tax reduction that is supposed to be temporary would actually turn out to be that in practice. But when a tax reduction is scheduled to last, let us say, just one year, many individuals will be more cautious in spending their larger after-tax income than if the lower taxes are expected to last indefinitely. Moreover, a temporary tax reduction, even if it applied to corporate as well as to personal incomes, would do little to strengthen the incentive of people to use their brains, energy, prior savings, or credit in enlarging their economic activity or that of the enterprises which they manage. Hence, a tax cut that is announced as temporary might well turn out to be permanent and yet have only a fraction of the stimulative power of a tax cut that is unencumbered by a time limitation.

In view of these difficulties with temporary tax cuts, it would be better to shape contracyclical tax policy in the context of a policy for economic growth. Two facts about our tax system need to be kept in mind in developing such a plan. First, despite some recent reductions, both individuals and corporations still carry a very heavy tax burden. In 1964, the tax revenues of our federal, state, and local governments amounted in the aggregate to 167 billion dollars, which was about 27 per cent of the gross national product. When we take account of depreciation in reckoning output, as indeed we should, it may fairly be said that taxes in 1964 took at least 30 per cent of the nation's total production of goods and services. The second major fact is that the federal part of our tax system is highly productive of revenue. When the economy grows at something like a normal rate, it is reasonable to expect that the existing structure of tax rates will add six or seven billion dollars a year to federal tax revenues. This means that we could reduce tax rates every year or nearly every year, and still have sufficient revenues to meet any modest increases in federal spending that may be needed.

I can think of no policy that is better designed to stimulate the long-term growth of the economy than a general rule of year-by-year reductions of tax rates. That, in effect, is what Japan has done in the post-war period, and the policy has worked remarkably well in that country. That is also what we ourselves have begun to do, although our future course has recently become clouded by the renewed upsurge of federal spending. At present, as I have sought to emphasize, the economy does not need any additional fiscal stimulus; but that happy condition will not continue indefinitely. To enable our economy to flourish and advance as it both can and should, further reductions of income tax rates will be needed. In another two years or so, if the budget is again nearly in balance, the federal government should be able to embark prudently on a systematic program of annual tax reductions. In order to do that, detailed legislative plans will have to be worked out earlier, and it is not too soon to begin.

The Congress has shown a willingness to pass tax legislation that is to take effect in a series of steps. This principle can be usefully extended. Thus, legislation might provide lower tax rates over the range of both personal and corporate incomes, the reductions proceeding annually over a period of, say, five years. The legislation, however, should permit some flexibility, and one way of doing this that may be acceptable to the Congress would be to stipulate that the reduction specified for a given fiscal year will not go into effect if the President decides that the national interest would be better served without it. In that event, however, the President should be required to inform the Congress of his decision, as well as the reasons for it, several weeks before the start of the new fiscal year, so that the Congress might have the opportunity, if it so chose, of overriding the presidential decision.

Tax legislation along these lines would serve to strengthen economic incentives throughout the economic community and therefore encourage enterprise, innovation, and investment. By applying a moderate but steady stimulus to the economy, it would provide some protection against both recession and inadequate growth. By giving the President a limited discretionary authority, it would provide some protection against inflation. By committing the nation to a moderately expansionist fiscal policy, it would facilitate a more active use of general credit restraints when they are needed to protect the balance of payments. Of course, economic circumstances of a future time may require stronger fiscal measures, whether to combat recession or to combat inflation or to offset credit restraints undertaken for international reasons. On an abstract plane, such needs could be met by broadening the range of presidential discretion. But I very much doubt whether the Congress or the nation will be willing to go beyond the minimum of delegated authority that I have suggested. And, in any event, the Congress can still act on whatever tax measures it may at any particular time deem suited to the nation's needs.

A long-term tax policy such as I have sketched would also help to keep in check the growth of federal expenditures. If a five-year federal tax program is desirable, so too are five-year budgets. Much too often new governmental programs have a low initial cost, but eventually grow far beyond what the Congress contemplated at the time of their adoption. Better control over federal expenditures would be achieved if probable costs were projected for several years, so that the Congress and the nation at large could judge more realistically the magnitude of the new undertakings together with the old. The need for prudence in federal spending is all the greater because of the pressing needs at the state and local level. Large cities across the nation are struggling with problems arising out of traffic congestion, air and water pollution, slums, and inadequate police protection. And the pressure is strong in small as well as large communities for more or better schools, roads, sanitary provisions, and welfare facilities. Lower federal tax rates would make it easier for state and local governments to finance their growing needs, and there would thus be less reason for the federal government to concern itself with activities that can usually be managed better on a decentralized basis.

The true test of any economic system is whether it betters human life. That is more than a matter of production, or prices, or employment. It involves also the freedom and the security of the individual. By and large, the American economy has met well the test of human betterment in our generation. We have

sixty-nine

preserved the essentials of economic and political freedom in a revolutionary age, when many other nations have lost or destroyed their freedom. Our economy has continued to grow in size and efficiency. The fruits of industry have been widely distributed among our people, so that poverty—as our parents once understood this condition—has been nearly eliminated in our country. We have made great strides in moderating the business cycle. Our future can be still better if we remain constantly alert to governmental economic policies, seek to improve them by being receptive to new economic ideas, and yet remain mindful of the teachings of experience about the vital importance of free markets, adequate economic incentives, and prudent management.

November 9, 1965

Fairless Memorial Lectures National Committee

James B. Black, *Chairman of the Board*
Pacific Gas and Electric Company
245 Market Street, San Francisco

Roger M. Blough, *Chairman of the Board*
United States Steel Corporation
525 William Penn Way, Pittsburgh

James M. Bovard, *President*
Carnegie Institute
4400 Forbes Avenue, Pittsburgh

Max D. Howell, *former President (retired)*
American Iron and Steel Institute
150 East Forty-Second Street, New York

George M. Humphrey, *Director*
National Steel Corporation
1300 Leader Building, Cleveland

George H. Love, *Chairman of the Board*
Consolidation Coal Company
Koppers Building, Pittsburgh

Richard K. Mellon, *Governor and President*
T. Mellon and Sons
Mellon Square, Pittsburgh

John P. Roche, *President*
American Iron and Steel Institute
150 East Forty-Second Street, New York

Edward L. Ryerson, *Honorary Director*
Inland Steel Company
30 West Monroe Street, Chicago

H. Guyford Stever, *President*
Carnegie Institute of Technology

John C. Warner, *President Emeritus*
Carnegie Institute of Technology

Charles M. White, *Director and Honorary Chairman*
Republic Steel Corporation
1511 Republic Building, Cleveland

Robert W. Woodruff, *formerly Chairman of the Board*
Coca Cola Company
Ichauway Plantation, Newton, Georgia